This
Scuba Diving Logbook
Belongs To:

_____

_____

_____

★ DIVE NO :	🗓 DATE:	⌚ TIME:
📍 LOCATION:	👥 DIVE GROUP:	⏱ DURATION:

WEATHER

🌡 _____   ☀   ⛅   🌧   ⛈   ❄   🎏   _____

OXYGEN CYLINDER CONDITIONS

START
bar / psi

_____

END
bar / psi

_____

DIVE LOCATION DETAILS

TIME IN

:

TIME OUT

:

DIVE TIME

:

AVERAGE DEPTH:

MAX DEPTH:

📓 NOTES:

★ DIVE NO :	📅 DATE:	⌚ TIME:
◎ LOCATION:	👥 DIVE GROUP:	⏱ DURATION:

WEATHER

🌡 _____ ☀ ⛅ 🌧 ⛈ ❄ 🎏 _____

OXYGEN CYLINDER CONDITIONS

START
bar / psi

_____

END
bar / psi

_____

DIVE LOCATION DETAILS

TIME IN
:

TIME OUT
:

DIVE TIME
:

AVERAGE DEPTH:

MAX DEPTH:

📝 NOTES:

_____

_____

_____

_____

_____

_____

_____

★ DIVE NO :	⊞ DATE:	〽 TIME:
⊙ LOCATION:	⚌ DIVE GROUP:	⏱ DURATION:

WEATHER

🌡 _____ ☀ ⛅ 🌧 ⛈ ❄ 🏳 _____

OXYGEN CYLINDER CONDITIONS

🛢	START bar / psi _____	🛢	END bar / psi _____

DIVE LOCATION DETAILS

TIME IN   TIME OUT

:   :

DIVE TIME

:

AVERAGE DEPTH:

MAX DEPTH:

📝 NOTES:

_____

_____

_____

_____

_____

_____

⭐ DIVE NO :	📅 DATE:	⌚ TIME:
📍 LOCATION:	👥 DIVE GROUP:	⏱ DURATION:

WEATHER

🌡 _____   ☀ 🌤 🌧 ⛈ ❄ 🚩 _____

OXYGEN CYLINDER CONDITIONS

START
bar / psi

_____

END
bar / psi

_____

DIVE LOCATION DETAILS

TIME IN

:

TIME OUT

:

DIVE TIME

:

AVERAGE DEPTH:

MAX DEPTH:

📟 NOTES:

_____

_____

_____

_____

_____

_____

⭐ DIVE NO :	📅 DATE:	⌚ TIME:
📍 LOCATION:	👥 DIVE GROUP:	⏱️ DURATION:

WEATHER

🌡️ _____   ☀️ ⛅ 🌧️ ⛈️ ❄️ 🎏 _____

OXYGEN CYLINDER CONDITIONS

START
bar / psi

_____

END
bar / psi

_____

DIVE LOCATION DETAILS

TIME IN
:

TIME OUT
:

DIVE TIME
:

AVERAGE DEPTH:

MAX DEPTH:

📝 NOTES:

_____

_____

_____

_____

_____

_____

| ★ DIVE NO : | 📅 DATE: | ⌚ TIME: |
| LOCATION: | 👥 DIVE GROUP: | ⏱ DURATION: |

WEATHER

🌡 _____ ☀ ⛅ ☁ ⛈ ❄ 🚩 _____

OXYGEN CYLINDER CONDITIONS

START
bar / psi

_____

END
bar / psi

_____

DIVE LOCATION DETAILS

TIME IN

:

TIME OUT

:

DIVE TIME

:

AVERAGE DEPTH:

MAX DEPTH:

📋 NOTES:

⭐ DIVE NO :	📅 DATE:	⌚ TIME:
📍 LOCATION:	👥 DIVE GROUP:	⏱️ DURATION:

WEATHER

🌡️ _____ ☀️ ⛅ 🌧️ ⛈️ ❄️ 🎏 _____

OXYGEN CYLINDER CONDITIONS

START
bar / psi

_____

END
bar / psi

_____

DIVE LOCATION DETAILS

TIME IN

:

TIME OUT

:

DIVE TIME

:

AVERAGE DEPTH:

MAX DEPTH:

📝 NOTES:

★ DIVE NO :	📅 DATE:	⌚ TIME:
📍 LOCATION:	👥 DIVE GROUP:	⏱ DURATION:

WEATHER

🌡 _____ ☀ ⛅ 🌧 ⛈ ❄ 🚩 _____

OXYGEN CYLINDER CONDITIONS

	START bar / psi		END bar / psi
	_____		_____

DIVE LOCATION DETAILS

TIME IN   TIME OUT

:   :

DIVE TIME

:

AVERAGE DEPTH:

MAX DEPTH:

📝 NOTES:

_____

_____

_____

_____

_____

_____

_____

★ DIVE NO :	🗓 DATE:	⌚ TIME:
⊙ LOCATION:	👥 DIVE GROUP:	⏱ DURATION:

WEATHER

🌡 _____   ☀   ⛅   ☁   🌧   ❄   🏴 _____

OXYGEN CYLINDER CONDITIONS

START
bar / psi

_____

END
bar / psi

_____

DIVE LOCATION DETAILS

TIME IN

:

TIME OUT

:

DIVE TIME

:

AVERAGE DEPTH:

MAX DEPTH:

📓 NOTES:

⭐ DIVE NO :	📅 DATE:	⏱ TIME:
📍 LOCATION:	👥 DIVE GROUP:	⏱ DURATION:

WEATHER

🌡 _____   ☀️ ⛅ 🌧 ⛈ ❄️ 🎏 _____

OXYGEN CYLINDER CONDITIONS

START
bar / psi

_____

END
bar / psi

_____

DIVE LOCATION DETAILS

TIME IN   TIME OUT

:   :

DIVE TIME

:

AVERAGE DEPTH:

MAX DEPTH:

📝 NOTES:

_____

_____

_____

_____

_____

_____

★ DIVE NO :	🗓 DATE:	⌚ TIME:
⊚ LOCATION:	👥 DIVE GROUP:	⏱ DURATION:

WEATHER

🌡 ____   ☀   ⛅   ☁   ⛈   ❄   🏳 ____

OXYGEN CYLINDER CONDITIONS

START
bar / psi

_____

END
bar / psi

_____

DIVE LOCATION DETAILS

TIME IN   TIME OUT

:   :

DIVE TIME

:

AVERAGE DEPTH:

MAX DEPTH:

📒 NOTES:

_____
_____
_____
_____
_____
_____
_____

★ DIVE NO :	📅 DATE:	⌚ TIME:
⊙ LOCATION:	👥 DIVE GROUP:	⏱ DURATION:

WEATHER

🌡 _____   ☀   ⛅   ☁   ⛈   ❄   🎏   _____

OXYGEN CYLINDER CONDITIONS

START bar / psi	END bar / psi
_____	_____

DIVE LOCATION DETAILS

TIME IN
:

TIME OUT
:

DIVE TIME
:

AVERAGE DEPTH:

MAX DEPTH:

NOTES:

★ DIVE NO :	🗓 DATE:	⌚ TIME:
⊙ LOCATION:	👥 DIVE GROUP:	⏱ DURATION:

WEATHER

🌡 _____   ☀ ⛅ 🌧 ⛈ ❄ 🎏 _____

OXYGEN CYLINDER CONDITIONS

START
bar / psi

_____

END
bar / psi

_____

DIVE LOCATION DETAILS

TIME IN
:

TIME OUT
:

DIVE TIME
:

AVERAGE DEPTH:

MAX DEPTH:

📋 NOTES:

_____

_____

_____

_____

_____

_____

★ DIVE NO :	📅 DATE:	⌚ TIME:
⦿ LOCATION:	👥 DIVE GROUP:	⏱ DURATION:

WEATHER

🌡 _____ ☀️ ⛅ 🌧 ⛈ ❄️ 🎏 _____

OXYGEN CYLINDER CONDITIONS

START
bar / psi

_____

END
bar / psi

_____

DIVE LOCATION DETAILS

TIME IN

:

TIME OUT

:

DIVE TIME

:

AVERAGE DEPTH:

MAX DEPTH:

📝 NOTES:

_____

_____

_____

_____

_____

_____

★ DIVE NO :	🗓 DATE:	⌚ TIME:
⊙ LOCATION:	👥 DIVE GROUP:	⏱ DURATION:

WEATHER

OXYGEN CYLINDER CONDITIONS

START
bar / psi

END
bar / psi

DIVE LOCATION DETAILS

TIME IN

TIME OUT

:

:

DIVE TIME

:

AVERAGE DEPTH:

MAX DEPTH:

📋 NOTES:

⭐ DIVE NO :	📅 DATE:	⌚ TIME:
◎ LOCATION:	👥 DIVE GROUP:	⏱ DURATION:

WEATHER

🌡 _____ ☀ 🌤 🌧 ⛈ ❄ 🎏 _____

OXYGEN CYLINDER CONDITIONS

START	END
bar / psi	bar / psi
_____	_____

DIVE LOCATION DETAILS

TIME IN   TIME OUT
:   :

DIVE TIME
:

AVERAGE DEPTH:

MAX DEPTH:

📄 NOTES:
_____
_____
_____
_____
_____
_____
_____

⭐ DIVE NO :	🗓 DATE:	⌚ TIME:
📍 LOCATION:	👥 DIVE GROUP:	⏱ DURATION:

WEATHER

🌡 _____ ☀ ⛅ 🌧 ⛈ ❄ 🚩 _____

OXYGEN CYLINDER CONDITIONS

START
bar / psi

_____

END
bar / psi

_____

DIVE LOCATION DETAILS

TIME IN

:

TIME OUT

:

DIVE TIME

:

AVERAGE DEPTH:

MAX DEPTH:

📝 NOTES:

_____

_____

_____

_____

_____

_____

★ DIVE NO :	📅 DATE:	⌚ TIME:
◎ LOCATION:	👥 DIVE GROUP:	⏱ DURATION:

WEATHER

🌡 _____ ☀ 🌤 ☁ ⛈ ❄ 🚩 _____

OXYGEN CYLINDER CONDITIONS

START
bar / psi

_____

END
bar / psi

_____

DIVE LOCATION DETAILS

TIME IN

:

TIME OUT

:

DIVE TIME

:

AVERAGE DEPTH:

MAX DEPTH:

📓 NOTES:

⭐ DIVE NO :	📅 DATE:	⌚ TIME:
📍 LOCATION:	👥 DIVE GROUP:	⏱️ DURATION:

WEATHER

OXYGEN CYLINDER CONDITIONS

START
bar / psi

END
bar / psi

DIVE LOCATION DETAILS

TIME IN

:

TIME OUT

:

DIVE TIME

:

AVERAGE DEPTH:

MAX DEPTH:

📝 NOTES:

★ DIVE NO :	📅 DATE:	⌚ TIME:
📍 LOCATION:	👥 DIVE GROUP:	⏱ DURATION:

WEATHER

🌡 _____ ☀️ ⛅ 🌧 ⛈ ❄️ 🚩 _____

OXYGEN CYLINDER CONDITIONS

START
bar / psi

_____

END
bar / psi

_____

DIVE LOCATION DETAILS

TIME IN

:

TIME OUT

:

DIVE TIME

:

AVERAGE DEPTH:

MAX DEPTH:

📝 NOTES:

_____

_____

_____

_____

_____

_____

★ DIVE NO :	🗓 DATE:	⌚ TIME:
◎ LOCATION:	👥 DIVE GROUP:	⏱ DURATION:

WEATHER

🌡 ____ ☀ ⛅ ☁🌧 ⛈ ❄ 🏴 ____

OXYGEN CYLINDER CONDITIONS

START
bar / psi

_____

END
bar / psi

_____

DIVE LOCATION DETAILS

TIME IN

:

TIME OUT

:

DIVE TIME

:

AVERAGE DEPTH:

MAX DEPTH:

📝 NOTES:

★ DIVE NO :	📅 DATE:	⌚ TIME:
◎ LOCATION:	👥 DIVE GROUP:	⏱ DURATION:

WEATHER

OXYGEN CYLINDER CONDITIONS

START
bar / psi

_____

END
bar / psi

_____

DIVE LOCATION DETAILS

TIME IN

:

TIME OUT

:

DIVE TIME

:

AVERAGE DEPTH:

MAX DEPTH:

📇 NOTES:

★ DIVE NO :	📅 DATE:	〰️ TIME:
📍 LOCATION:	👥 DIVE GROUP:	⏱️ DURATION:

WEATHER

🌡️ _____   ☀️ ⛅ ☁️ ⛈️ ❄️ 🚩 _____

OXYGEN CYLINDER CONDITIONS

START
bar / psi

_____

END
bar / psi

_____

DIVE LOCATION DETAILS

TIME IN

:

TIME OUT

:

DIVE TIME

:

AVERAGE DEPTH:

MAX DEPTH:

📝 NOTES:

★ DIVE NO :	📅 DATE:	⌚ TIME:
📍 LOCATION:	👥 DIVE GROUP:	⏱ DURATION:

WEATHER

🌡 ____   ☀   ⛅   ☁   ⛈   ❄   🏳 ____

OXYGEN CYLINDER CONDITIONS

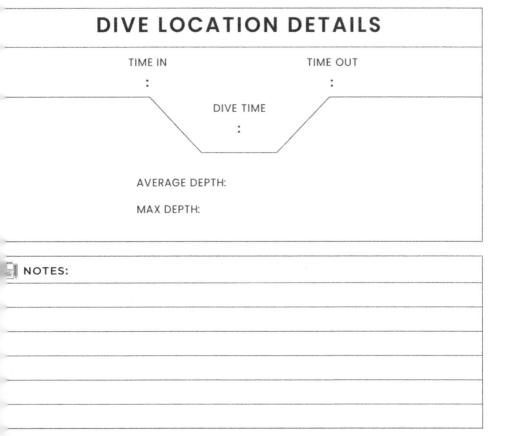

START
bar / psi

_____

END
bar / psi

_____

DIVE LOCATION DETAILS

TIME IN   TIME OUT

:   :

DIVE TIME

:

AVERAGE DEPTH:

MAX DEPTH:

NOTES:

⭐ DIVE NO :	📅 DATE:	⌚ TIME:
📍 LOCATION:	👥 DIVE GROUP:	⏱ DURATION:

WEATHER

🌡 _____   ☀️   ⛅   🌧   ⛈   ❄️   🎐 _____

OXYGEN CYLINDER CONDITIONS

START
bar / psi

_____

END
bar / psi

_____

DIVE LOCATION DETAILS

TIME IN

:

TIME OUT

:

DIVE TIME

:

AVERAGE DEPTH:

MAX DEPTH:

📝 NOTES:

★ DIVE NO :	📅 DATE:	⌚ TIME:
📍 LOCATION:	👥 DIVE GROUP:	⏱ DURATION:

WEATHER

🌡 _____ ☀️ ⛅ 🌧 ⛈ ❄️ 🎏 _____

OXYGEN CYLINDER CONDITIONS

START
bar / psi

_____

END
bar / psi

_____

DIVE LOCATION DETAILS

TIME IN
:

TIME OUT
:

DIVE TIME
:

AVERAGE DEPTH:

MAX DEPTH:

📝 NOTES:

_____

_____

_____

_____

_____

_____

★ DIVE NO :	📅 DATE:	⌚ TIME:
📍 LOCATION:	👥 DIVE GROUP:	⏱ DURATION:

WEATHER

🌡 _____ ☀️ ⛅ 🌧 ⛈ ❄️ 🎏 _____

OXYGEN CYLINDER CONDITIONS

START
bar / psi

_____

END
bar / psi

_____

DIVE LOCATION DETAILS

TIME IN

:

TIME OUT

:

DIVE TIME

:

AVERAGE DEPTH:

MAX DEPTH:

📝 NOTES:

★ DIVE NO :	📅 DATE:	⌚ TIME:
◎ LOCATION:	👥 DIVE GROUP:	⏱ DURATION:

WEATHER

🌡 _____   ☀ ⛅ 🌧 ⛈ ❄ 🎏 _____

OXYGEN CYLINDER CONDITIONS

START
bar / psi

_____

END
bar / psi

_____

DIVE LOCATION DETAILS

TIME IN   TIME OUT

:   :

DIVE TIME

:

AVERAGE DEPTH:

MAX DEPTH:

📝 NOTES:

_____
_____
_____
_____
_____
_____
_____

⭐ DIVE NO :	📅 DATE:	⌚ TIME:
📍 LOCATION:	👥 DIVE GROUP:	⏱️ DURATION:

WEATHER

🌡️ _____ ☀️ ⛅ 🌧️ ⛈️ ❄️ 🎏 _____

OXYGEN CYLINDER CONDITIONS

START
bar / psi

_____

END
bar / psi

_____

DIVE LOCATION DETAILS

TIME IN

:

TIME OUT

:

DIVE TIME

:

AVERAGE DEPTH:

MAX DEPTH:

📓 NOTES:

★ DIVE NO :	🗓 DATE:	⌚ TIME:
⊚ LOCATION:	👥 DIVE GROUP:	⏱ DURATION:

WEATHER

🌡 _____   ☀ 🌤 ☁ ⛈ ❄ 🚩 _____

OXYGEN CYLINDER CONDITIONS

START	END
bar / psi	bar / psi
_____	_____

DIVE LOCATION DETAILS

TIME IN   TIME OUT

:   :

DIVE TIME

:

AVERAGE DEPTH:

MAX DEPTH:

📝 NOTES:

_____

_____

_____

_____

_____

_____

★ DIVE NO :	📅 DATE:	⌚ TIME:
◎ LOCATION:	👥 DIVE GROUP:	⏱ DURATION:

WEATHER

🌡 _____ ☀ 🌤 🌧 ⛈ ❄ 🎏 _____

OXYGEN CYLINDER CONDITIONS

START
bar / psi

_____

END
bar / psi

_____

DIVE LOCATION DETAILS

TIME IN :

TIME OUT :

DIVE TIME :

AVERAGE DEPTH:

MAX DEPTH:

📝 NOTES:

⭐ DIVE NO :	📅 DATE:	⌚ TIME:
📍 LOCATION:	👥 DIVE GROUP:	⏱️ DURATION:

WEATHER

🌡️ _____ ☀️ ⛅ ☁️ 🌧️ ❄️ 🚩 _____

OXYGEN CYLINDER CONDITIONS

🛢️	START bar / psi _____	END bar / psi _____

DIVE LOCATION DETAILS

TIME IN
:

TIME OUT
:

DIVE TIME
:

AVERAGE DEPTH:

MAX DEPTH:

📝 NOTES:

_____
_____
_____
_____
_____
_____
_____

⭐ DIVE NO :	📅 DATE:	⌚ TIME:
📍 LOCATION:	👥 DIVE GROUP:	⏱️ DURATION:

WEATHER

🌡️ _____ ☀️ ⛅ ☁️ ⛈️ ❄️ 🏳️ _____

OXYGEN CYLINDER CONDITIONS

START
bar / psi

_____

END
bar / psi

_____

DIVE LOCATION DETAILS

TIME IN

:

TIME OUT

:

DIVE TIME

:

AVERAGE DEPTH:

MAX DEPTH:

📝 NOTES:

⭐ DIVE NO :	📅 DATE:	⌚ TIME:
📍 LOCATION:	👥 DIVE GROUP:	⏱️ DURATION:

WEATHER

🌡️ _____   ☀️   ⛅   🌧️   ⛈️   ❄️   🚩 _____

OXYGEN CYLINDER CONDITIONS

START
bar / psi

_____

END
bar / psi

_____

DIVE LOCATION DETAILS

TIME IN

:

TIME OUT

:

DIVE TIME

:

AVERAGE DEPTH:

MAX DEPTH:

📝 NOTES:

★ DIVE NO :	📅 DATE:	⌚ TIME:
📍 LOCATION:	👥 DIVE GROUP:	⏱ DURATION:

WEATHER

🌡 _____   ☀ ⛅ ☁ ⛈ ❄ 🚩 _____

OXYGEN CYLINDER CONDITIONS

START
bar / psi

_____

END
bar / psi

_____

DIVE LOCATION DETAILS

TIME IN   TIME OUT

:   :

DIVE TIME

:

AVERAGE DEPTH:

MAX DEPTH:

📝 NOTES:

★ DIVE NO :	🗓 DATE:	⌚ TIME:
⊙ LOCATION:	👥 DIVE GROUP:	⏱ DURATION:

WEATHER

🌡 _____ ☀ 🌤 🌧 ⛈ ❄ 🚩 _____

OXYGEN CYLINDER CONDITIONS

START
bar / psi

_____

END
bar / psi

_____

DIVE LOCATION DETAILS

TIME IN
:

TIME OUT
:

DIVE TIME
:

AVERAGE DEPTH:

MAX DEPTH:

🗒 NOTES:

_____

_____

_____

_____

_____

_____

_____

★ DIVE NO :	📅 DATE:	⌚ TIME:
📍 LOCATION:	👥 DIVE GROUP:	⏱ DURATION:

WEATHER

🌡 _____ ☀ ⛅ 🌧 ⛈ ❄ 🎏 _____

OXYGEN CYLINDER CONDITIONS

START
bar / psi

_____

END
bar / psi

_____

DIVE LOCATION DETAILS

TIME IN   TIME OUT

:   :

DIVE TIME

:

AVERAGE DEPTH:

MAX DEPTH:

📝 NOTES:

_____

_____

_____

_____

_____

_____

★ DIVE NO :	📅 DATE:	⌚ TIME:
◎ LOCATION:	👥 DIVE GROUP:	⏱ DURATION:

WEATHER

🌡 _____ ☀ ⛅ 🌧 ⛈ ❄ 🚩 _____

OXYGEN CYLINDER CONDITIONS

START
bar / psi

_____

END
bar / psi

_____

DIVE LOCATION DETAILS

TIME IN

:

TIME OUT

:

DIVE TIME

:

AVERAGE DEPTH:

MAX DEPTH:

📝 NOTES:

★ DIVE NO :	🗓 DATE:	⌚ TIME:
◎ LOCATION:	👥 DIVE GROUP:	⏱ DURATION:

WEATHER

🌡 ____ ☀ ⛅ ☁ ⛈ ❄ 🚩 ____

OXYGEN CYLINDER CONDITIONS

START
bar / psi

____

END
bar / psi

____

DIVE LOCATION DETAILS

TIME IN
:

TIME OUT
:

DIVE TIME
:

AVERAGE DEPTH:

MAX DEPTH:

📝 NOTES:

⭐ DIVE NO :	📅 DATE:	⌚ TIME:
📍 LOCATION:	👥 DIVE GROUP:	⏱ DURATION:

WEATHER

🌡 _____   ☀️   ⛅   🌧   ⛈   ❄️   🚩 _____

OXYGEN CYLINDER CONDITIONS

START bar / psi	END bar / psi
_____	_____

DIVE LOCATION DETAILS

TIME IN :

TIME OUT :

DIVE TIME :

AVERAGE DEPTH:

MAX DEPTH:

📓 NOTES:

_____

_____

_____

_____

_____

_____

_____

⭐ DIVE NO :	📅 DATE:	⌚ TIME:
📍 LOCATION:	👥 DIVE GROUP:	⏱ DURATION:

WEATHER

🌡 _____   ☀ 🌤 🌥 ⛈ ❄ 🎏 _____

OXYGEN CYLINDER CONDITIONS

START
bar / psi

_____

END
bar / psi

_____

DIVE LOCATION DETAILS

TIME IN
:

TIME OUT
:

DIVE TIME
:

AVERAGE DEPTH:

MAX DEPTH:

📓 NOTES:

_____
_____
_____
_____
_____
_____
_____

★ DIVE NO :	🗓 DATE:	⌚ TIME:
◎ LOCATION:	👥 DIVE GROUP:	⏱ DURATION:

WEATHER

🌡 _____ ☀ ⛅ 🌧 ⛈ ❄ 🚩 _____

OXYGEN CYLINDER CONDITIONS

START
bar / psi

_____

END
bar / psi

_____

DIVE LOCATION DETAILS

TIME IN

:

TIME OUT

:

DIVE TIME

:

AVERAGE DEPTH:

MAX DEPTH:

📝 NOTES:

_____

_____

_____

_____

_____

_____

_____

⭐ DIVE NO :	📅 DATE:	⌚ TIME:
📍 LOCATION:	👥 DIVE GROUP:	⏱ DURATION:

WEATHER

🌡 _____   ☀️   ⛅   🌧   ⛈   ❄️   🎏 _____

OXYGEN CYLINDER CONDITIONS

START
bar / psi

_____

END
bar / psi

_____

DIVE LOCATION DETAILS

TIME IN

:

TIME OUT

:

DIVE TIME

:

AVERAGE DEPTH:

MAX DEPTH:

📝 NOTES:

★ DIVE NO :	📅 DATE:	⌚ TIME:
📍 LOCATION:	👥 DIVE GROUP:	⏱ DURATION:

WEATHER

🌡 _____ ☀ ⛅ ☁ ⛈ ❄ 🚩 _____

OXYGEN CYLINDER CONDITIONS

START
bar / psi

_____

END
bar / psi

_____

DIVE LOCATION DETAILS

TIME IN

:

TIME OUT

:

DIVE TIME

:

AVERAGE DEPTH:

MAX DEPTH:

📝 NOTES:

_____

_____

_____

_____

_____

_____

_____

⭐ DIVE NO :	📅 DATE:	⌚ TIME:
📍 LOCATION:	👥 DIVE GROUP:	⏱ DURATION:

WEATHER

🌡 _____ ☀️ ⛅ ☁️ ⛈ ❄️ 🎏 _____

OXYGEN CYLINDER CONDITIONS

START
bar / psi

_____

END
bar / psi

_____

DIVE LOCATION DETAILS

TIME IN

:

TIME OUT

:

DIVE TIME

:

AVERAGE DEPTH:

MAX DEPTH:

📝 NOTES:

★ DIVE NO :	📅 DATE:	⌚ TIME:
📍 LOCATION:	👥 DIVE GROUP:	⏱ DURATION:

WEATHER

🌡 _____   ☀️ ⛅ 🌧 ⛈ ❄️ 🚩 _____

OXYGEN CYLINDER CONDITIONS

START
bar / psi

_____

END
bar / psi

_____

DIVE LOCATION DETAILS

TIME IN

:

TIME OUT

:

DIVE TIME

:

AVERAGE DEPTH:

MAX DEPTH:

📝 NOTES:

_____

_____

_____

_____

_____

_____

_____

★ DIVE NO :	📅 DATE:	⌚ TIME:
📍 LOCATION:	👥 DIVE GROUP:	⏱️ DURATION:

WEATHER

🌡️ _____ ☀️ ⛅ ☁️🌧️ ⛈️ ❄️ 🚩 _____

OXYGEN CYLINDER CONDITIONS

START
bar / psi

_____

END
bar / psi

_____

DIVE LOCATION DETAILS

TIME IN
:

TIME OUT
:

DIVE TIME
:

AVERAGE DEPTH:

MAX DEPTH:

📋 NOTES:

_____

_____

_____

_____

_____

_____

| ★ DIVE NO : | 📅 DATE: | ⌚ TIME: |
| LOCATION: | 👥 DIVE GROUP: | ⏱ DURATION: |

WEATHER

| 🌡 | _____ | ☀ | ⛅ | 🌧 | ⛈ | ❄ | 🏳 | _____ |

OXYGEN CYLINDER CONDITIONS

START
bar / psi

_____

END
bar / psi

_____

DIVE LOCATION DETAILS

TIME IN

:

TIME OUT

:

DIVE TIME

:

AVERAGE DEPTH:

MAX DEPTH:

🗒 NOTES:

★ DIVE NO :	📅 DATE:	⌚ TIME:
📍 LOCATION:	👥 DIVE GROUP:	⏱ DURATION:

WEATHER

OXYGEN CYLINDER CONDITIONS

START
bar / psi

END
bar / psi

DIVE LOCATION DETAILS

TIME IN

:

TIME OUT

:

DIVE TIME

:

AVERAGE DEPTH:

MAX DEPTH:

📝 NOTES:

★ DIVE NO :	🗓 DATE:	⌚ TIME:
◎ LOCATION:	👥 DIVE GROUP:	⏱ DURATION:

WEATHER

🌡 _____   ☀   ⛅   ☁   ⛈   ❄   🚩 _____

OXYGEN CYLINDER CONDITIONS

START bar / psi	END bar / psi
_____	_____

DIVE LOCATION DETAILS

TIME IN

:

TIME OUT

:

DIVE TIME

:

AVERAGE DEPTH:

MAX DEPTH:

📝 NOTES:

_____

_____

_____

_____

_____

_____

★ DIVE NO :	📅 DATE:	⌚ TIME:
📍 LOCATION:	👥 DIVE GROUP:	⏱ DURATION:

WEATHER

🌡 _____ ☀️ ⛅ ☁️🌧 ⛈ ❄️ 🚩 _____

OXYGEN CYLINDER CONDITIONS

START
bar / psi

_____

END
bar / psi

_____

DIVE LOCATION DETAILS

TIME IN   TIME OUT

:   :

DIVE TIME

:

AVERAGE DEPTH:

MAX DEPTH:

📝 NOTES:

⭐ DIVE NO :	📅 DATE:	⌚ TIME:
📍 LOCATION:	👥 DIVE GROUP:	⏱ DURATION:

WEATHER

🌡 _____   ☀️ ⛅ ☁️🌧 ⛈ ❄️ 🎏 _____

OXYGEN CYLINDER CONDITIONS

START
bar / psi

_____

END
bar / psi

_____

DIVE LOCATION DETAILS

TIME IN

:

TIME OUT

:

DIVE TIME

:

AVERAGE DEPTH:

MAX DEPTH:

📓 NOTES:

_____

_____

_____

_____

_____

_____

_____

★ DIVE NO :	📅 DATE:	⌚ TIME:
📍 LOCATION:	👥 DIVE GROUP:	⏱ DURATION:

WEATHER

OXYGEN CYLINDER CONDITIONS

START
bar / psi

END
bar / psi

DIVE LOCATION DETAILS

TIME IN

:

TIME OUT

:

DIVE TIME

:

AVERAGE DEPTH:

MAX DEPTH:

📓 NOTES:

★ DIVE NO :	🗓 DATE:	⌚ TIME:
◎ LOCATION:	👥 DIVE GROUP:	⏱ DURATION:

WEATHER

🌡 _____   ☀️   ⛅   ☁️   ⛈   ❄️   🎐   _____

OXYGEN CYLINDER CONDITIONS

START bar / psi	END bar / psi
_____	_____

DIVE LOCATION DETAILS

TIME IN   TIME OUT

:   :

DIVE TIME

:

AVERAGE DEPTH:

MAX DEPTH:

NOTES:

⭐ DIVE NO :	📅 DATE:	⌚ TIME:
📍 LOCATION:	👥 DIVE GROUP:	⏱ DURATION:

WEATHER

🌡 _____ ☀ ⛅ 🌧 ⛈ ❄ 🎏 _____

OXYGEN CYLINDER CONDITIONS

START
bar / psi

_____

END
bar / psi

_____

DIVE LOCATION DETAILS

TIME IN
:

TIME OUT
:

DIVE TIME
:

AVERAGE DEPTH:

MAX DEPTH:

📝 NOTES:

★ DIVE NO :	📅 DATE:	⌚ TIME:
◎ LOCATION:	👥 DIVE GROUP:	⏱ DURATION:

WEATHER

🌡 _____   ☀   ⛅   ☁   🌧   ❄   🎏 _____

OXYGEN CYLINDER CONDITIONS

START
bar / psi

_____

END
bar / psi

_____

DIVE LOCATION DETAILS

TIME IN

:

TIME OUT

:

DIVE TIME

:

AVERAGE DEPTH:

MAX DEPTH:

📰 NOTES:

_____

_____

_____

_____

_____

_____

_____

★ DIVE NO :	📅 DATE:	⌚ TIME:
📍 LOCATION:	👥 DIVE GROUP:	⏱ DURATION:

WEATHER

OXYGEN CYLINDER CONDITIONS

START
bar / psi

_____

END
bar / psi

_____

DIVE LOCATION DETAILS

TIME IN   TIME OUT

:   :

DIVE TIME

:

AVERAGE DEPTH:

MAX DEPTH:

📝 NOTES:

⭐ DIVE NO :	📅 DATE:	⌚ TIME:
📍 LOCATION:	👥 DIVE GROUP:	⏱ DURATION:

WEATHER

🌡 ____   ☀️ ⛅ ☁️ 🌧 ❄️ 🚩 ____

OXYGEN CYLINDER CONDITIONS

	START		END
	bar / psi		bar / psi
	_____		_____

DIVE LOCATION DETAILS

TIME IN :   TIME OUT :

DIVE TIME :

AVERAGE DEPTH:

MAX DEPTH:

📓 NOTES:

_____
_____
_____
_____
_____
_____
_____

★ DIVE NO :	📅 DATE:	⌚ TIME:
📍 LOCATION:	👥 DIVE GROUP:	⏱ DURATION:

WEATHER

🌡 ____   ☀ ⛅ ☁ ⛈ ❄ 🚩 ____

OXYGEN CYLINDER CONDITIONS

START
bar / psi

_____

END
bar / psi

_____

DIVE LOCATION DETAILS

TIME IN

:

TIME OUT

:

DIVE TIME

:

AVERAGE DEPTH:

MAX DEPTH:

📝 NOTES:

_____

_____

_____

_____

_____

★ DIVE NO :	📅 DATE:	⌚ TIME:
◎ LOCATION:	👥 DIVE GROUP:	⏱ DURATION:

WEATHER

🌡 _____ ☀️ ⛅ 🌧 ⛈ ❄️ 🎏 _____

OXYGEN CYLINDER CONDITIONS

START
bar / psi

_____

END
bar / psi

_____

DIVE LOCATION DETAILS

TIME IN

:

TIME OUT

:

DIVE TIME

:

AVERAGE DEPTH:

MAX DEPTH:

📑 NOTES:

_____

_____

_____

_____

_____

_____

_____

⭐ DIVE NO :	📅 DATE:	⌚ TIME:
📍 LOCATION:	👥 DIVE GROUP:	⏱️ DURATION:

WEATHER

🌡️ _____   ☀️   ⛅   🌧️   ⛈️   ❄️   🎏 _____

OXYGEN CYLINDER CONDITIONS

START
bar / psi

_____

END
bar / psi

_____

DIVE LOCATION DETAILS

TIME IN
:

TIME OUT
:

DIVE TIME
:

AVERAGE DEPTH:

MAX DEPTH:

📝 NOTES:

★ DIVE NO :	📅 DATE:	⌚ TIME:
📍 LOCATION:	👥 DIVE GROUP:	⏱ DURATION:

WEATHER

🌡 _____ ☀ ⛅ ☁ 🌧 ⛈ ❄ 🚩 _____

OXYGEN CYLINDER CONDITIONS

START
bar / psi

_____

END
bar / psi

_____

DIVE LOCATION DETAILS

TIME IN

:

TIME OUT

:

DIVE TIME

:

AVERAGE DEPTH:

MAX DEPTH:

📓 NOTES:

_____

_____

_____

_____

_____

_____

_____

★ DIVE NO :	🗓 DATE:	⌚ TIME:
📍 LOCATION:	👥 DIVE GROUP:	⏱ DURATION:

WEATHER

🌡 _____   ☀   ⛅   ☁   ⛈   ❄   🎐   _____

OXYGEN CYLINDER CONDITIONS

START
bar / psi

_____

END
bar / psi

_____

DIVE LOCATION DETAILS

TIME IN

:

TIME OUT

:

DIVE TIME

:

AVERAGE DEPTH:

MAX DEPTH:

📓 NOTES:

_____

_____

_____

_____

_____

_____

★ DIVE NO :	📅 DATE:	⌚ TIME:
◎ LOCATION:	👥 DIVE GROUP:	⏱ DURATION:

WEATHER

🌡 _____ ☀ ⛅ ☁ 🌧 ❄ 🚩 _____

OXYGEN CYLINDER CONDITIONS

START
bar / psi

_____

END
bar / psi

_____

DIVE LOCATION DETAILS

TIME IN

:

TIME OUT

:

DIVE TIME

:

AVERAGE DEPTH:

MAX DEPTH:

📝 NOTES:

_____

_____

_____

_____

_____

_____

_____

★ DIVE NO :	📅 DATE:	⌚ TIME:
📍 LOCATION:	👥 DIVE GROUP:	⏱ DURATION:

WEATHER

🌡 _____   ☀️ ⛅ 🌧 ⛈ ❄️ 🚩 _____

OXYGEN CYLINDER CONDITIONS

START
bar / psi

_____

END
bar / psi

_____

DIVE LOCATION DETAILS

TIME IN

:

TIME OUT

:

DIVE TIME

:

AVERAGE DEPTH:

MAX DEPTH:

📝 NOTES:

★ DIVE NO :	🗓 DATE:	⌚ TIME:
⊙ LOCATION:	👥 DIVE GROUP:	⏱ DURATION:

WEATHER

🌡 _____   ☀ ⛅ 🌧 ⛈ ❄ 🎏 _____

OXYGEN CYLINDER CONDITIONS

START
bar / psi

_____

END
bar / psi

_____

DIVE LOCATION DETAILS

TIME IN

:

TIME OUT

:

DIVE TIME

:

AVERAGE DEPTH:

MAX DEPTH:

📋 NOTES:

_____

_____

_____

_____

_____

_____

★ DIVE NO :	📅 DATE:	⌚ TIME:
📍 LOCATION:	👥 DIVE GROUP:	⏱ DURATION:

WEATHER

OXYGEN CYLINDER CONDITIONS

START
bar / psi

END
bar / psi

DIVE LOCATION DETAILS

TIME IN

TIME OUT

:

:

DIVE TIME

:

AVERAGE DEPTH:

MAX DEPTH:

📝 NOTES:

★ DIVE NO :	📅 DATE:	⌚ TIME:
◎ LOCATION:	👥 DIVE GROUP:	⏱ DURATION:

WEATHER

🌡 _____   ☀️ ⛅ ☁️ 🌧 ❄️ 🚩 _____

OXYGEN CYLINDER CONDITIONS

START
bar / psi

_____

END
bar / psi

_____

DIVE LOCATION DETAILS

TIME IN
:

TIME OUT
:

DIVE TIME
:

AVERAGE DEPTH:

MAX DEPTH:

📓 NOTES:

★ DIVE NO :	📅 DATE:	⌚ TIME:
📍 LOCATION:	👥 DIVE GROUP:	⏱ DURATION:

WEATHER

🌡 _____ ☀ ⛅ ☁ ⛈ ❄ 🚩 _____

OXYGEN CYLINDER CONDITIONS

START
bar / psi

_____

END
bar / psi

_____

DIVE LOCATION DETAILS

TIME IN

:

TIME OUT

:

DIVE TIME

:

AVERAGE DEPTH:

MAX DEPTH:

📝 NOTES:

⭐ DIVE NO :	📅 DATE:	⌚ TIME:
📍 LOCATION:	👥 DIVE GROUP:	⏱ DURATION:

WEATHER

🌡 _____   ☀️ ⛅ ☁️ 🌧 ⛈ ❄️ 🚩 _____

OXYGEN CYLINDER CONDITIONS

START
bar / psi

_____

END
bar / psi

_____

DIVE LOCATION DETAILS

TIME IN

:

TIME OUT

:

DIVE TIME

:

AVERAGE DEPTH:

MAX DEPTH:

📓 NOTES:

_____

_____

_____

_____

_____

_____

_____

★ DIVE NO :	📅 DATE:	⌚ TIME:
📍 LOCATION:	👥 DIVE GROUP:	⏱ DURATION:

WEATHER

🌡 _____ ☀ ⛅ ☁ ⛈ ❄ 🚩 _____

OXYGEN CYLINDER CONDITIONS

START
bar / psi

_____

END
bar / psi

_____

DIVE LOCATION DETAILS

TIME IN

:

TIME OUT

:

DIVE TIME

:

AVERAGE DEPTH:

MAX DEPTH:

📝 NOTES:

★ DIVE NO :	🗓 DATE:	⌚ TIME:
◎ LOCATION:	👥 DIVE GROUP:	⏱ DURATION:

WEATHER

🌡 _____ ☀ ⛅ ☁ ⛈ ❄ 🚩 _____

OXYGEN CYLINDER CONDITIONS

START bar / psi	END bar / psi
_____	_____

DIVE LOCATION DETAILS

TIME IN   TIME OUT

:   :

DIVE TIME

:

AVERAGE DEPTH:

MAX DEPTH:

NOTES:

_____

_____

_____

_____

_____

_____

_____

★ DIVE NO :	📅 DATE:	⌚ TIME:
📍 LOCATION:	👥 DIVE GROUP:	⏱ DURATION:

WEATHER

🌡 _____ ☀️ ⛅ 🌧 ⛈ ❄️ 🎏 _____

OXYGEN CYLINDER CONDITIONS

START
bar / psi

_____

END
bar / psi

_____

DIVE LOCATION DETAILS

TIME IN

:

TIME OUT

:

DIVE TIME

:

AVERAGE DEPTH:

MAX DEPTH:

📝 NOTES:

★ DIVE NO :	📅 DATE:	⌚ TIME:
◎ LOCATION:	👥 DIVE GROUP:	⏱ DURATION:

WEATHER

🌡 ____ ☀ 🌤 ☁ 🌧 ⛈ ❄ 🎐 ____

OXYGEN CYLINDER CONDITIONS

	START bar / psi		END bar / psi
	_____		_____

DIVE LOCATION DETAILS

TIME IN :

TIME OUT :

DIVE TIME :

AVERAGE DEPTH:

MAX DEPTH:

📝 NOTES:

_____

_____

_____

_____

_____

_____

_____

★ DIVE NO :	📅 DATE:	⌚ TIME:
📍 LOCATION:	👥 DIVE GROUP:	⏱ DURATION:

WEATHER

🌡 _____   ☀ ⛅ ☁ ⛈ ❄ 🎏 _____

OXYGEN CYLINDER CONDITIONS

START
bar / psi

_____

END
bar / psi

_____

DIVE LOCATION DETAILS

TIME IN :

TIME OUT :

DIVE TIME :

AVERAGE DEPTH:

MAX DEPTH:

📓 NOTES:

★ DIVE NO :	📅 DATE:	⌚ TIME:
◎ LOCATION:	👥 DIVE GROUP:	⏱ DURATION:

WEATHER

🌡 _____ ☀ ⛅ ☁ ⛈ ❄ 🎏 _____

OXYGEN CYLINDER CONDITIONS

START bar / psi	END bar / psi
_____	_____

DIVE LOCATION DETAILS

TIME IN :

TIME OUT :

DIVE TIME :

AVERAGE DEPTH:

MAX DEPTH:

📓 NOTES:

_____

_____

_____

_____

_____

_____

_____

★ DIVE NO :	📅 DATE:	⌚ TIME:
📍 LOCATION:	👥 DIVE GROUP:	⏱ DURATION:

WEATHER

OXYGEN CYLINDER CONDITIONS

START
bar / psi

END
bar / psi

DIVE LOCATION DETAILS

TIME IN

TIME OUT

:

:

DIVE TIME

:

AVERAGE DEPTH:

MAX DEPTH:

📓 NOTES:

| ★ DIVE NO : | 📅 DATE: | ⌚ TIME: |
| LOCATION: | 👥 DIVE GROUP: | ⏱ DURATION: |

WEATHER

🌡 _____ ☀ ⛅ 🌧 ⛈ ❄ 🚩 _____

OXYGEN CYLINDER CONDITIONS

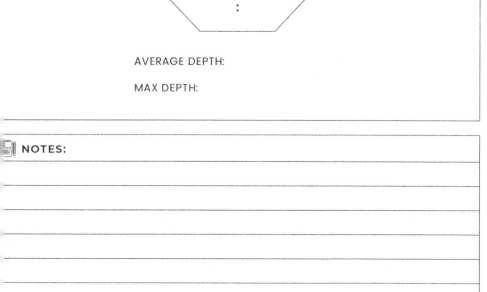

START
bar / psi

_____

END
bar / psi

_____

DIVE LOCATION DETAILS

TIME IN
:

TIME OUT
:

DIVE TIME
:

AVERAGE DEPTH:

MAX DEPTH:

📓 NOTES:

_____

_____

_____

_____

_____

_____

★ DIVE NO :	📅 DATE:	⌚ TIME:
📍 LOCATION:	👥 DIVE GROUP:	⏱ DURATION:

WEATHER

🌡 ____ ☀ 🌤 🌧 ⛈ ❄ 🎏 ____

OXYGEN CYLINDER CONDITIONS

START
bar / psi

_____

END
bar / psi

_____

DIVE LOCATION DETAILS

TIME IN :

TIME OUT :

DIVE TIME :

AVERAGE DEPTH:

MAX DEPTH:

📝 NOTES:

★ DIVE NO :	🗓 DATE:	⌚ TIME:
◎ LOCATION:	👥 DIVE GROUP:	⏱ DURATION:

WEATHER

🌡 _____ ☀ ⛅ ☁ ⛈ ❄ 🎏 _____

OXYGEN CYLINDER CONDITIONS

	START bar / psi		END bar / psi
	_____		_____

DIVE LOCATION DETAILS

TIME IN

:

TIME OUT

:

DIVE TIME

:

AVERAGE DEPTH:

MAX DEPTH:

📝 NOTES:

_____

_____

_____

_____

_____

_____

★ DIVE NO :	📅 DATE:	⌚ TIME:
📍 LOCATION:	👥 DIVE GROUP:	⏱ DURATION:

WEATHER

🌡 _____ ☀ ⛅ ☁ 🌧 ⛈ ❄ 🚩 _____

OXYGEN CYLINDER CONDITIONS

START
bar / psi

_____

END
bar / psi

_____

DIVE LOCATION DETAILS

TIME IN :

TIME OUT :

DIVE TIME :

AVERAGE DEPTH:

MAX DEPTH:

📓 NOTES:

⭐ DIVE NO :	📅 DATE:	⌚ TIME:
📍 LOCATION:	👥 DIVE GROUP:	⏱ DURATION:

WEATHER

🌡 _____ ☀ ⛅ ☁ 🌧 ❄ 🚩 _____

OXYGEN CYLINDER CONDITIONS

	START bar / psi		END bar / psi
🛢	_____	🛢	_____

DIVE LOCATION DETAILS

TIME IN
:

TIME OUT
:

DIVE TIME
:

AVERAGE DEPTH:

MAX DEPTH:

📝 NOTES:

_____

_____

_____

_____

_____

_____

★ DIVE NO :	📅 DATE:	⌚ TIME:
◎ LOCATION:	👥 DIVE GROUP:	⏱ DURATION:

WEATHER

🌡 ____   ☀️ ⛅ ☁️ 🌧 ❄️ 🚩 ____

OXYGEN CYLINDER CONDITIONS

START
bar / psi

____

END
bar / psi

____

DIVE LOCATION DETAILS

TIME IN
:

TIME OUT
:

DIVE TIME
:

AVERAGE DEPTH:

MAX DEPTH:

📓 NOTES:

★ DIVE NO :	🗓 DATE:	⌚ TIME:
◎ LOCATION:	👥 DIVE GROUP:	⏱ DURATION:

WEATHER

🌡 ____   ☀ ⛅ 🌧 ⛈ ❄ 🎏 ____

OXYGEN CYLINDER CONDITIONS

START bar / psi	END bar / psi
____	____

DIVE LOCATION DETAILS

TIME IN
:

TIME OUT
:

DIVE TIME
:

AVERAGE DEPTH:

MAX DEPTH:

NOTES:

⭐ DIVE NO :	📅 DATE:	⌚ TIME:
📍 LOCATION:	👥 DIVE GROUP:	⏱ DURATION:

WEATHER

🌡 _____   ☀ ⛅ 🌧 ⛈ ❄ 🎏 _____

OXYGEN CYLINDER CONDITIONS

START
bar / psi

_____

END
bar / psi

_____

DIVE LOCATION DETAILS

TIME IN
:

TIME OUT
:

DIVE TIME
:

AVERAGE DEPTH:

MAX DEPTH:

📝 NOTES:

⭐ DIVE NO :	📅 DATE:	⌚ TIME:
📍 LOCATION:	👥 DIVE GROUP:	⏱️ DURATION:

WEATHER

🌡️ _____   ☀️   ⛅   ☁️   🌧️   ❄️   🚩 _____

OXYGEN CYLINDER CONDITIONS

	START bar / psi		END bar / psi
	_____		_____

DIVE LOCATION DETAILS

TIME IN   TIME OUT

:   :

DIVE TIME

:

AVERAGE DEPTH:

MAX DEPTH:

📝 NOTES:

_____

_____

_____

_____

_____

_____

★ DIVE NO :	🗓 DATE:	⌚ TIME:
◉ LOCATION:	👥 DIVE GROUP:	⏱ DURATION:

WEATHER

🌡 ____ ☀ 🌤 ☁🌧 ⛈ ❄ 🏴 ____

OXYGEN CYLINDER CONDITIONS

START
bar / psi

_____

END
bar / psi

_____

DIVE LOCATION DETAILS

TIME IN

:

TIME OUT

:

DIVE TIME

:

AVERAGE DEPTH:

MAX DEPTH:

📝 NOTES:

⭐ DIVE NO :	📅 DATE:	⌚ TIME:
📍 LOCATION:	👥 DIVE GROUP:	⏱️ DURATION:

WEATHER

🌡️ 〰️ ☀️ ⛅ ☁️ 🌧️ ❄️ 🚩 〰️

OXYGEN CYLINDER CONDITIONS

START
bar / psi

_____

END
bar / psi

_____

DIVE LOCATION DETAILS

TIME IN

:

TIME OUT

:

DIVE TIME

:

AVERAGE DEPTH:

MAX DEPTH:

📓 NOTES:

_____

_____

_____

_____

_____

_____

★ DIVE NO :	📅 DATE:	⌚ TIME:
📍 LOCATION:	👥 DIVE GROUP:	⏱ DURATION:

WEATHER

🌡 _____ ☀ ⛅ ☁ 🌧 ❄ 🚩 _____

OXYGEN CYLINDER CONDITIONS

START
bar / psi

_____

END
bar / psi

_____

DIVE LOCATION DETAILS

TIME IN

:

TIME OUT

:

DIVE TIME

:

AVERAGE DEPTH:

MAX DEPTH:

📝 NOTES:

★ DIVE NO :	🗓 DATE:	⌚ TIME:
⦿ LOCATION:	👥 DIVE GROUP:	⏱ DURATION:

WEATHER

🌡 _____   ☀ ⛅ 🌧 ⛈ ❄ 🚩 _____

OXYGEN CYLINDER CONDITIONS

START
bar / psi

_____

END
bar / psi

_____

DIVE LOCATION DETAILS

TIME IN   TIME OUT

:   :

DIVE TIME

:

AVERAGE DEPTH:

MAX DEPTH:

📓 NOTES:

_____

_____

_____

_____

_____

_____

_____

⭐ DIVE NO :	📅 DATE:	⌚ TIME:
📍 LOCATION:	👥 DIVE GROUP:	⏱ DURATION:

WEATHER

🌡 _____   ☀️   ⛅   🌧   ⛈   ❄️   🚩 _____

OXYGEN CYLINDER CONDITIONS

START
bar / psi

_____

END
bar / psi

_____

DIVE LOCATION DETAILS

TIME IN :   TIME OUT :

DIVE TIME :

AVERAGE DEPTH:

MAX DEPTH:

📝 NOTES:

_____
_____
_____
_____
_____
_____
_____

★ DIVE NO :	📅 DATE:	⌚ TIME:
📍 LOCATION:	👥 DIVE GROUP:	⏱ DURATION:

WEATHER

🌡 _____   ☀️   ⛅   ☁️   🌧   ❄️   🎏 _____

OXYGEN CYLINDER CONDITIONS

START
bar / psi

_____

END
bar / psi

_____

DIVE LOCATION DETAILS

TIME IN

:

TIME OUT

:

DIVE TIME

:

AVERAGE DEPTH:

MAX DEPTH:

📝 NOTES:

_____
_____
_____
_____
_____
_____
_____

★ DIVE NO :	📅 DATE:	⌚ TIME:
📍 LOCATION:	👥 DIVE GROUP:	⏱ DURATION:

WEATHER

🌡 _____   ☀ ⛅ ☁ ⛈ ❄ 🎏 _____

OXYGEN CYLINDER CONDITIONS

START
bar / psi

_____

END
bar / psi

_____

DIVE LOCATION DETAILS

TIME IN

:

TIME OUT

:

DIVE TIME

:

AVERAGE DEPTH:

MAX DEPTH:

📝 NOTES:

⭐ DIVE NO :	📅 DATE:	⌚ TIME:
📍 LOCATION:	👥 DIVE GROUP:	⏱️ DURATION:

WEATHER

🌡️ _____ ☀️ ⛅ ☁️ 🌧️ ❄️ 🎏 _____

OXYGEN CYLINDER CONDITIONS

START
bar / psi
_____

END
bar / psi
_____

DIVE LOCATION DETAILS

TIME IN
:

TIME OUT
:

DIVE TIME
:

AVERAGE DEPTH:

MAX DEPTH:

📝 NOTES:

★ DIVE NO :	📅 DATE:	⌚ TIME:
📍 LOCATION:	👥 DIVE GROUP:	⏱ DURATION:

WEATHER

🌡 _____   ☀️ ⛅ ☁️ ⛈ ❄️ 🎏 _____

OXYGEN CYLINDER CONDITIONS

START
bar / psi

_____

END
bar / psi

_____

DIVE LOCATION DETAILS

TIME IN

:

TIME OUT

:

DIVE TIME

:

AVERAGE DEPTH:

MAX DEPTH:

📓 NOTES:

DIVE NO :	DATE:	TIME:
LOCATION:	DIVE GROUP:	DURATION:

WEATHER

OXYGEN CYLINDER CONDITIONS

START
bar / psi

_____

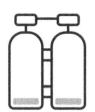

END
bar / psi

_____

DIVE LOCATION DETAILS

TIME IN

:

TIME OUT

:

DIVE TIME

:

AVERAGE DEPTH:

MAX DEPTH:

NOTES:

_____

_____

_____

_____

_____

_____

★ DIVE NO :	📅 DATE:	⌚ TIME:
◎ LOCATION:	👥 DIVE GROUP:	⏱ DURATION:

WEATHER

🌡 _____ ☀ ⛅ 🌧 ⛈ ❄ 🎏 _____

OXYGEN CYLINDER CONDITIONS

START
bar / psi

_____

END
bar / psi

_____

DIVE LOCATION DETAILS

TIME IN

:

TIME OUT

:

DIVE TIME

:

AVERAGE DEPTH:

MAX DEPTH:

📝 NOTES:

_____
_____
_____
_____
_____
_____
_____

★ DIVE NO :	📅 DATE:	⌚ TIME:
◎ LOCATION:	👥 DIVE GROUP:	⏱ DURATION:

WEATHER

🌡 _____ ☀ ⛅ ☁ 🌧 ❄ 🚩 _____

OXYGEN CYLINDER CONDITIONS

START
bar / psi

_____

END
bar / psi

_____

DIVE LOCATION DETAILS

TIME IN

:

TIME OUT

:

DIVE TIME

:

AVERAGE DEPTH:

MAX DEPTH:

📝 NOTES:

_____

_____

_____

_____

_____

_____

★ DIVE NO :	📅 DATE:	⌚ TIME:
◎ LOCATION:	👥 DIVE GROUP:	⏱ DURATION:

WEATHER

🌡 _____   ☀   ⛅   ☁   🌧   ❄   🎏 _____

OXYGEN CYLINDER CONDITIONS

START
bar / psi

_____

END
bar / psi

_____

DIVE LOCATION DETAILS

TIME IN   :

TIME OUT   :

DIVE TIME   :

AVERAGE DEPTH:

MAX DEPTH:

📝 NOTES:

⭐ DIVE NO :	📅 DATE:	⌚ TIME:
📍 LOCATION:	👥 DIVE GROUP:	⏱ DURATION:

WEATHER

🌡 _____ ☀ ⛅ ☁ 🌧 ⛈ ❄ 🎏 _____

OXYGEN CYLINDER CONDITIONS

START
bar / psi

_____

END
bar / psi

_____

DIVE LOCATION DETAILS

TIME IN

:

TIME OUT

:

DIVE TIME

:

AVERAGE DEPTH:

MAX DEPTH:

📓 NOTES:

★ DIVE NO :	🗓 DATE:	⌚ TIME:
◉ LOCATION:	👥 DIVE GROUP:	⏱ DURATION:

WEATHER

🌡 _____ ☀ ⛅ ☁ 🌧 ❄ 🎏 _____

OXYGEN CYLINDER CONDITIONS

START
bar / psi

_____

END
bar / psi

_____

DIVE LOCATION DETAILS

TIME IN

:

TIME OUT

:

DIVE TIME

:

AVERAGE DEPTH:

MAX DEPTH:

📝 NOTES:

★ DIVE NO :	📅 DATE:	⌚ TIME:
◎ LOCATION:	👥 DIVE GROUP:	⏱ DURATION:

WEATHER

🌡 ____ ☀ ⛅ 🌧 ⛈ ❄ 🚩 ____

OXYGEN CYLINDER CONDITIONS

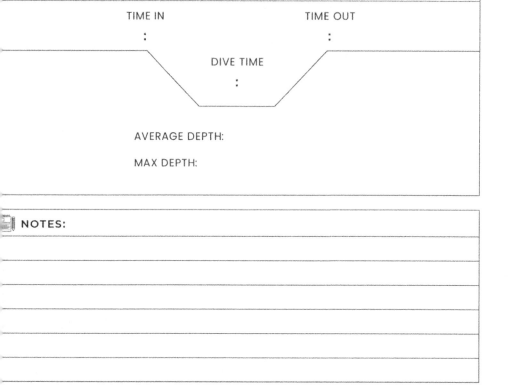

START
bar / psi

_____

END
bar / psi

_____

DIVE LOCATION DETAILS

TIME IN

:

TIME OUT

:

DIVE TIME

:

AVERAGE DEPTH:

MAX DEPTH:

📠 NOTES:

★ DIVE NO :	🗓 DATE:	⌚ TIME:
◎ LOCATION:	👥 DIVE GROUP:	⏱ DURATION:

WEATHER

🌡 _____ ☀ 🌤 ☁ 🌧 ⛈ ❄ 🎏 _____

OXYGEN CYLINDER CONDITIONS

START
bar / psi

_____

END
bar / psi

_____

DIVE LOCATION DETAILS

TIME IN

:

TIME OUT

:

DIVE TIME

:

AVERAGE DEPTH:

MAX DEPTH:

📝 NOTES:

★ DIVE NO :	🗓 DATE:	⌚ TIME:
◎ LOCATION:	👥 DIVE GROUP:	⏱ DURATION:

WEATHER

🌡 _____ ☀ ⛅ ☁ 🌧 ❄ 🎏 _____

OXYGEN CYLINDER CONDITIONS

	START bar / psi	
	_____	
	END bar / psi	
	_____	

DIVE LOCATION DETAILS

TIME IN

:

TIME OUT

:

DIVE TIME

:

AVERAGE DEPTH:

MAX DEPTH:

📝 NOTES:

⭐ DIVE NO :	📅 DATE:	⌚ TIME:
📍 LOCATION:	👥 DIVE GROUP:	⏱️ DURATION:

WEATHER

🌡️ _____   ☀️   ⛅   ☁️   🌧️   ⛈️   ❄️   🎏 _____

OXYGEN CYLINDER CONDITIONS

START
bar / psi

_____

END
bar / psi

_____

DIVE LOCATION DETAILS

TIME IN   TIME OUT

:   :

DIVE TIME

:

AVERAGE DEPTH:

MAX DEPTH:

📝 NOTES:

_____
_____
_____
_____
_____
_____

⭐ DIVE NO :	📅 DATE:	⌚ TIME:
◎ LOCATION:	👥 DIVE GROUP:	⏱ DURATION:

WEATHER

🌡 _____ ☀ ⛅ ☁ 🌧 ❄ 🚩 _____

OXYGEN CYLINDER CONDITIONS

START
bar / psi
_____

END
bar / psi
_____

DIVE LOCATION DETAILS

TIME IN   TIME OUT
:   :

DIVE TIME
:

AVERAGE DEPTH:

MAX DEPTH:

📓 NOTES:

⭐ DIVE NO :	📅 DATE:	⌚ TIME:
📍 LOCATION:	👥 DIVE GROUP:	⏱️ DURATION:

WEATHER

🌡️ _____ ☀️ ⛅ ☁️ ⛈️ ❄️ 🎐 _____

OXYGEN CYLINDER CONDITIONS

START
bar / psi

_____

END
bar / psi

_____

DIVE LOCATION DETAILS

TIME IN

:

TIME OUT

:

DIVE TIME

:

AVERAGE DEPTH:

MAX DEPTH:

📓 NOTES:

★ DIVE NO :	📅 DATE:	⌚ TIME:
◎ LOCATION:	👥 DIVE GROUP:	⏱ DURATION:

WEATHER

🌡 _____ ☀ ⛅ 🌧 ⛈ ❄ 🚩 _____

OXYGEN CYLINDER CONDITIONS

START
bar / psi

_____

END
bar / psi

_____

DIVE LOCATION DETAILS

TIME IN   TIME OUT

:   :

DIVE TIME

:

AVERAGE DEPTH:

MAX DEPTH:

📝 NOTES:

_____

_____

_____

_____

_____

_____

_____

⭐ DIVE NO :	📅 DATE:	⌚ TIME:
📍 LOCATION:	👥 DIVE GROUP:	⏱️ DURATION:

WEATHER

🌡️ _____ ☀️ ⛅ ☁️ 🌧️ ⛈️ ❄️ 🚩 _____

OXYGEN CYLINDER CONDITIONS

	START bar / psi		END bar / psi
	_____		_____

DIVE LOCATION DETAILS

TIME IN

:

TIME OUT

:

DIVE TIME

:

AVERAGE DEPTH:

MAX DEPTH:

📝 NOTES:

Made in the USA
Monee, IL
17 December 2022

22242881R00066